JUST ONE

DEBORAH STRICKLIN

Newberry, FL 32669

Bridge-Logos, Inc.
Newberry, FL 32669

Just One: One Purpose, One Body, One God.
by Deborah Stricklin

Library of Congress Catalog Card Number: 2025949003

International Standard Book Number: 978-1-61036-924-4

International Standard Book Number: 979-8815-0969-9

Interior Layout and Cover Design:
Ashley Morgan | GraphicGardenLLC@gmail.com

CONTENTS

FOREWORD

It is a true privilege to introduce you to the latest work of Deborah Stricklin, whose writing continues to challenge, uplift, and inspire all who read her words. In this book, Deborah once again demonstrates her remarkable ability to take us on a journey of reflection, urging us to see beyond the immediate and consider the eternal.

The pages you hold in your hands are the product of years spent in quiet communion with the Father, and these words carry the weight of deep spiritual insight and a life lived in humble obedience. If I were to choose one passage that shows the heartbeat of this book, it would be Ephesians 4:4-6: *"There is one body and one Spirit, just as you were called to one hope when you were called; one Lord, one faith, one baptism; one God and Father of all, who is over all and through all and in all" (NIV).*

Through her words, Deborah calls us to remember the uniqueness of our faith, the unity of the body of Christ, and the unwavering truth of one God who is over all. In a world that seems to be splintering in every direction, her message is a clarion call to return to the basics—one Lord, one faith, one baptism, and one God who reigns supreme.

Deborah doesn't just ask us to consider these truths; she challenges us to live them out in a world that is increasingly unfamiliar with such faithfulness. With authenticity and wisdom, she directs us away from our current cultural message, urging us to walk in righteousness and remembrance of our eternal purpose. One of the most powerful thoughts in the book is this: *"The shedding of our pride and self-sufficiency through developing true dependence on Him gives His grace a wide berth in our lives to change us."* It's a call to embrace humility and surrender, recognizing that only by leaning into Him can we experience true transformation.

I have had the privilege of knowing Deborah for many years, and I've watched firsthand as she has lived out these countercultural principles. This is not a book of theoretical advice; it is a record of wisdom, shaped by decades of walking with God through the highs and lows of life. Deborah's life itself is a testimony to the principles she writes about—she lives with eternity in mind, and her choices today are made with the understanding that they will ripple through generations to come.

When we choose to live with a generational perspective, we begin to recognize that every decision we make today has the power to either bless or bind future generations. This book reminds us of that profound truth and encourages us to align our lives with eternal priorities. As you read, you will be invited to consider how you are living today, and how your choices are shaping the legacy you will leave for tomorrow.

Each book Deborah writes opens my eyes in new ways, helping me to rediscover the peace and freedom that come from remaining in His presence. This book is no different. If you long to stay focused on your one true purpose—exalting Him—if you want to be reminded that as a believer in Jesus, you are part of a unified body, and if you long to live with the knowledge that there is only one God, then I implore you to read this book and reflect on its message again and again.

Deborah, thank you for your unwavering commitment to truth, for your sacrificial love for the Lord, and for your willingness to share your wisdom with us. You have once again provided us with a roadmap for living out our faith with purpose and passion.

—**SHEILA L. HARPER,** Founder/President SaveOne,
Author & International Speaker

INTRODUCTION

In a society that values individualism, we often need to be reminded that we are part of a Kingdom that functions best in community. In Christ, we are one body with one purpose—to honor Him with our lives. Let the words of this book serve as an instructive challenge to us, the Body of Christ, to create forward movement in His Kingdom through unity and purpose. There is just one: one purpose, one body, one God.

> *For there is one body and one Spirit, just as you have been called to one glorious hope for the future. There is one Lord, one faith, one baptism, one God and Father of all, who is over all, in all, and living through all.*
>
> (Ephesians 4:4-6)

Chapter 1

THE GOSPEL MESSAGE

A sovereign (noun) is defined as one who has the highest authority and is controlled by no one else. An earthly king is often called a sovereign. Somehow, we've come to believe that our political and religious freedom have earned us the right to be our own sovereigns. It seems that our independent, opinionated lives have created a society full of people who want to control others with their opinions but be controlled by no one—not even God.

God is the only true Sovereign. We, as human beings, were created to work together to serve the purposes of the Sovereign God. Although we have been given extraordinary minds to think, reason, and create, we are misusing what we've been granted to instead serve ourselves.

The Gospel Message is one of suffering and sacrifice. Father God assigned His Son Jesus Christ to leave the beauty and rulership of heaven to be born among the most ordinary of humanity. Growing up under the authority of human parents, Scripture teaches us that Jesus learned obedience. Although He was himself God, Jesus asserted none of His rights as Sovereign and instead subjugated himself to the rulers of this world. And even though He became our High Priest through His death and resurrection, while on this earth He had no access to the office of priesthood.

In every way, He chose to limit himself for the purpose of being our example of serving His heavenly Father. When Jesus took on human flesh, He chose to endure the humiliation, tears, and loss of this earthly life, leaving behind the honor, exaltation, and perfection of heaven.

As humans, we naturally tend toward self-service and self-exaltation. The sin nature we were born with lends itself to self-focus. Consequently, we often believe that we're somehow owed a favored life with unlimited possibilities. Social media has taken this human tendency to a whole new level of egocentrism. The desire for more and more followers and viral status often drives people to create a life-platform centered on recognition. And with increased recognition comes the belief that the life we created will continue to increasingly deliver fame, satisfaction, and monetary reward—in effect, a limitless life.

We find ourselves striving to live limitless lives, but our definition of limitless involves throwing off control and exerting our independence. Jesus' example to us is very much in opposition to this idea of throwing off control. He willingly humbled himself, stepping away from His rightful place in heaven in order to offer *us* full access to His Father. Our desire, our goal, our purpose should be to humble ourselves before our Sovereign and come together to serve Him. Jesus' death on a cross was the fullest expression of sacrifice that could ever be given, and yet we treat the Gospel Message as a license for freedom to create lives of ease and self-importance.

The Gospel Message is meant to serve as an example of humility and sacrifice. It's one of willingness to suffer for the purposes of a higher authority. But we've lost sight of our purpose and are not truly serving Him. We've chosen instead to serve ourselves. Jesus combatted this human tendency over and over as He walked the earth. He confronted the self-righteous religious leaders and spoke pointedly to human rulers.

Jesus—the Master Communicator—had a way of speaking just the right words to cut to the quick. No heart was completely immune to His pointed words. Some leaders followed Him to challenge His actions and find fault with Him. Many others were intrigued by His words and followed Him to hear His teaching. And still others followed Him to benefit from His many miracles. But Jesus had a way of revealing the true motivation in each person's heart. John chapter six gives us a clear picture of Jesus' method of exposing the hearts of His listeners.

Huge crowds of people had been following Jesus, and this particular day was no different. As Jesus sat with His twelve disciples, a large crowd of people came near. *"Turning to Philip, he asked, 'Where can we buy bread to feed all these people?' He was testing Philip, for he already knew what he was going to do"* (John 6:5b-6). Jesus, using a little boy's lunch, prayed over the loaves and fish and proceeded to distribute the food among the thousands of people present. Everyone ate their fill.

Having displayed His deity through the miraculous multiplication of fish and loaves, the crowd wanted to make Jesus their leader—their king. Jesus knew their fascination with Him was based on what He could give them, not on His identity as Sovereign. He wasn't enticed by their desire to exalt Him, and He quietly slipped away. Jesus' twelve disciples waited until nightfall for Jesus to return to the shore, but when He didn't come, they left in a boat without Him to go to the other side of the lake.

In the morning, when the people realized Jesus had departed, they went looking for Him. They weren't looking for the Sovereign to whom they would humbly submit; they were seeking the One who could provide for their immediate needs —specifically to satiate their hunger and heal their bodies. When they finally found Jesus, He began teaching them by giving them some difficult concepts. He challenged their misplaced exaltation of Moses and then spoke of His own body being food and His blood being drink. The people were offended by His words, and many who had been following Him for His teaching began to walk away. At that point, Jesus turned to His closest companions—The Twelve—and asked, *"Are you also going to leave? Simon Peter replied, 'Lord, to whom would we go? You have the words that give eternal life. We believe, and we know you are the Holy One of God'"* (John 6:67-68). Indeed, Jesus is the Christ, the Holy One of God.

My heart yearns for a fuller understanding of our Sovereign and a greater willingness to humble myself to His purposes. This posture of surrender and humility is in great opposition to the attitudes and heart position of many people around us. Although the contrast between service to self and service to Sovereign is not unique to our time in history, our cooperation in making this heart-change is critically needed today.

A powerful, life-changing question is: What could God do with a people who are fully submitted to Him and focused on *His* purposes throughout the earth? The possibilities are truly limitless because we serve a God who is limitless. Quite honestly, I want to experience the answer to that question.

Several years ago, I began an experiment—saying yes to God without reservation. Rather than filtering God's instructions to me through my own reasoning, I decided to simply say yes to Him without knowing *how* He would accomplish His purposes through my life. I realize that saying yes sounds like an obvious response to the Almighty God—our Sovereign—but I was effectively making the choice to push everything and everyone else off the throne of my heart. I wanted to learn to follow Him wholeheartedly whether I understood His leading or not, whether I had explanation for His instructions or not. That kind of living flies in the face of the self-made life. And, quite honestly, in many ways, it opposes our westernized concept of the Christian life.

As a people begin to trust God and obey His ways, in time His gracious blessings often follow. In our self-focused human nature, those blessings tend to become our object of affection rather than the One who bestowed those blessings upon us. Inevitably, we begin to view our blessed lives as our rightful reward, and somehow the Gospel Message becomes about us instead of Christ.

The blessings that come our way as we follow the principles outlined in God's Word are meant to be not only a joy to us but also a resource to bless the watching world. All too easily, we begin to spend those heavenly resources on ourselves. But God is calling us back to the Message of sacrifice and humility—to the true Gospel of the Sovereign One which is marked by submission and surrender.

As we avail ourselves to the life-giving Message of the finished work of Jesus Christ, Father God entrusts us with sharing this message with those around us. We tend to see ourselves as door-to-door salesmen of the Gospel, but I think God primarily intends us to be living examples set ablaze by the power of the Holy Spirit. Rather than simply talking about the transformational power of the Gospel of Jesus Christ, we must be transformed by it and exemplify its power by our Spirit-filled lives.

When we're filled up with His Spirit, boldness and miraculous signs should be an earmark of our submitted lives. Jesus said to His disciples,

> *"Go into all the world and preach the Good News to everyone. Anyone who believes and is baptized will be saved. But anyone who refuses to believe will be condemned. These miraculous signs will accompany those who believe: They will cast out demons in my name, and they will speak in new languages. They will be able to handle snakes with safety, and if they drink anything poisonous, it won't hurt them. They will be able to place their hands on the sick, and they will be healed." When the Lord Jesus had finished talking with them, he was taken up into heaven and sat down in the place of honor at God's right hand.* (Mark 16:17-19)

And this is our assignment as well—to preach the Good News with our Spirit-filled lives.

Jesus' work was complete. He lived as our example, gave us our assignment and then returned to His Father in Heaven. What He left us to accomplish is no small task—*Go into all the world and preach the Good News to everyone.* But the key to accomplishing it is total submission and complete surrender. If we remain in control of our own lives, we cannot accomplish the task. If we will walk with Him in submission and surrender, He can accomplish the task through us. When onlookers see these miraculous signs at work in our lives, they come face-to-face with the reality that God's Kingdom is here. And they're challenged with the choice to surrender the throne of their hearts or remain self-ruled.

The Good News is that the Kingdom of heaven has arrived among us and now lives within us. There is no partiality; the Kingdom is available to everyone. But one important question is: Can the world tell the difference between those who have received and appropriated the Good News and those who have not? As Christians, our lives should be markedly different. The miraculous signs mentioned by Mark should be evident in our lives. But are they? By looking too much like the world around us, we diminish the attractiveness of the Gospel. The power of the Gospel Message itself is never diminished because of the finished work of Jesus Christ, but our lives mask its attractiveness when we live powerless lives.

Living powerless Christian lives reminds me of the parable of the soils from Matthew 13—specifically the third type of soil. I imagine you've heard the parable before: The Sower (Christ/disciples of Christ) goes out to sow seed (the Good News of Jesus Christ), and the seed falls on four types of soil (the human heart). The first type of soil is hard and impenetrable. The second is shallow with bedrock too close to the surface. The seed sown into the third soil is interspersed with other plants—mostly briers and thistles. And the fourth type of soil is fertile—potentially producing a huge harvest.

Although every type of soil has pertinent application to our lives, I am particularly interested in the third type of soil. Matthew 13:7 says that *"Other seeds fell among thorns that grew up and choked out the tender plants."* And Jesus' subsequent explanation of the parable to His disciples gives us more information. *"The seed that fell among the thorns represents those who hear God's word, but all too quickly the message is crowded out by the worries of this life and the lure of wealth, so no fruit is produced"* (v. 22).

The third type of soil is essentially a hotbed of competition for love and loyalty. I imagine when the Good News is first planted in this type of heart, it is received joyfully. It takes time for the importance of the Message to grow to maturity in the human heart. But by the time the young plant should be maturing in this third type of soil, the thorns and briers have grown up as well. And the competition for priority heightens. The plants vie for the available water and nutrients. And by the laws of nature, the most aggressive plant assuredly wins.

As we allow our lives to be filled up with worldly cares and concerns, we give too much attention to temporal affections and not enough attention to the eternal. "Cares" can be anything that attracts our attention and draws us away from focusing on our eternal purpose: the satisfying things in life, the exciting moments, the disappointments, and the painful experiences. In effect, anything that consistently diverts our attention away from the eternal becomes a competing love. It's admittedly challenging to live in a world that we're called not to get too attached to. But our response should be to aggressively uproot those cares that compete for our affections.

We must choose to surrender our affections for the "cares" of this life and submit our hearts fully to the Sovereign One. As we begin to view our lives as either submitted to man's kingdom (focused on the temporal) or God's Kingdom (focused on the eternal), we become more aware that we cannot live in the middle between them. We must choose. And the effectiveness of our lives for the Kingdom of God depends on our choice.

There is just One King—just One Sovereign. And He demands (and deserves) complete loyalty from those who have accepted His Gospel Message.

Chapter 2

RELATIONSHIPS

The Gospel Message is one of community and inter-connectedness, valuing others above self. The apostle Paul, in his letter to the believers in Ephesus, spoke of the Gospel as a mystery—the coming together of Jew and Gentile, of the old and new—revealed through the sacrifice of Jesus Christ. *"This mystery is that the Gentiles are fellow heirs, members of the same body, and partakers of the promise in Christ Jesus through the gospel"* (Ephesians 3:6, ESV).

Paul continues to press the point of oneness in the Body of Christ, *"For there is one body and one Spirit, just as you have been called to one glorious hope for the future. There is one Lord, one faith, one baptism, one God and Father of all, who is over all, in all, and living through all"* (Ephesians 4:4-6).

The Gospel Message is unique among world religions. Other religions that boast connectedness to God emphasize man striving toward reconciliation with God. But the Gospel Message is about God coming toward man to offer reconciliation because of His great love for us. Jesus Christ—the Son of God—became one of us to give us access to the Father. And the proverbial icing on the cake is that we have the third person of the Trinity—the Holy Spirit—residing in us to facilitate close relationship with the Father.

While Jesus was here on earth, He *"shouted to the crowds"* gathered at the Jewish Festival of Shelters, "*'Anyone who is thirsty may come to me! Anyone who believes in me may come and drink! For the Scriptures declare, 'Rivers of living water will flow from his heart.' (When he said 'living water,' he was speaking of the Spirit, who would be given to everyone believing in him. But the Spirit had not yet been given, because Jesus had not yet entered into his glory)*" (John 7:37-39).

Regarding Jesus' words *"For the Scriptures declare,"* He is not pointing to a single reference but rather many prophetic references throughout Scripture to the life-giving water (Spirit) at work in the hearts of believers. Here are a couple of examples:

> *But now, listen to me, Jacob my servant, Israel my chosen one. The Lord who made you and helps you says: Do not be afraid, O Jacob, my servant, O dear Israel, my chosen one. For I will pour out water to quench your thirst and to irrigate your parched fields. And I will pour out my Spirit on your descendants, and my blessing on your children. They will thrive like watered grass, like willows on a riverbank.*
>
> (Isaiah 44:1-4)

> *How precious is your unfailing love, O God! All humanity finds shelter in the shadow of your wings. You feed them from the abundance of your own house, letting them drink from your river of delights. For you are the fountain of life, the light by which we see.* (Psalm 36:7-9)

How we steward that precious Living Water flowing through us is important. The prophet Jeremiah spoke on the Lord's behalf, reminding Judah that they had become self-reliant and that what they'd trusted in would fail. *"For my people have done two evil things: They have abandoned me—the fountain of living water. And they have dug for themselves cracked cisterns that can hold no water at all"* (Jeremiah 2:13). Cisterns are not self-sustaining. They are reliant on rainwater, and God was telling the people of Judah that their source would dry up. But if they would put their trust in God, He is a constant Source of Living Water.

What was promised in the Old Testament and given in the New Testament will forever be available to us in the New Jerusalem.

> *Then the angel showed me a river with the water of life, clear as crystal, flowing from the throne of God and of the Lamb. It flowed down the center of the main street. On each side of the river grew a tree of life, bearing twelve crops of fruit, with a fresh crop each month. The leaves were used for medicine to heal the nations.* (Revelation 22:1)

What an incredibly beautiful plan Father God has accomplished! The Living Water that flows both into us and out of us gives life everywhere we go. And one day, we'll experience the ultimate fulfillment of this Water as we are in the presence of God.

We most certainly do not understand the enormous potential this Water offers us today! Imagine the dryness of a hot desert; what would be the value of a cold glass of drinking water to someone walking in that desert? Or imagine an athlete completing a long race; what would be the value of a large bottle of water to the thirsty competitor? That refreshing drink would be priceless. Some people know they're thirsty—thirsty for the life-giving Water of Jesus Christ. They just don't know *how* to satiate their thirst. But still others don't know that they're actually dehydrated—their bodies are slowly dying of thirst.

We, as Spirit-filled believers in Jesus Christ, carry the life-giving Water that others need. I know we've often heard those words in church, but perhaps we don't realize the magnitude of the implications of those words. Picture yourself pouring out this life-giving Water everywhere you go. There's a green swath of Life left in your wake. Others benefit from the Life you bring. Their eyes are open to the possibility that God actually sees them and cares about their lives. Through us, God creates life-giving opportunities each day, everywhere we set our feet.

I frequently take walks through my neighborhood. Yes, I'm exercising my physical body, and I'm often praying as I walk. But I see my frequent walks as a beautiful gift of Life to each occupant of our subdivision. It's not about the prayers I pray as I walk, although those can be powerful. It's about the presence of the Living God that resides in me bringing Life to my neighbors. I may not be able to see it in the natural, but that Life is like a refreshing rain my neighbors need. They may not know why they suddenly experience a breath of fresh air as I walk by, but the Holy Spirit is bringing it nonetheless.

When we bring the Life of Christ wherever we go, the enemy's minions have to respond; most likely they'll want to get out of the area—away from the presence of the Almighty God in us. People near us can then experience clarity and peace that may be markedly different from their chaotic or clouded thinking. Do we see ourselves as that kind of catalyst? Unfortunately, most of us Christians haven't viewed ourselves as a powerful catalyst for the Kingdom. And it's not because we're somehow powerful in ourselves; it's because of the Living Water present in us.

Much of our concept of relationships has to do with how we think others view us. But what if we stop considering ourselves and instead think about how Christ's presence through us is affecting those around us? We are the catalyst of change that the world around us needs. By the power of the Holy Spirit, we are conduits of Life. We bring refreshing, life-giving Water to those around us. We are a catalyst for God's Kingdom!

We are also reminded in the New Testament by the apostle Paul that we are interconnected in the Body of Christ. Our relationships with one another are critical to our understanding of Jesus as the Head and us as the Body. One part of the body cannot function without the other parts of the body. And the body cannot function without the Head bringing order and direction. Our independent, western mindset often hinders us from seeing ourselves as dependent on one another. But when we link arms with our brothers and sisters in Christ, we begin to experience an infusion of Life that is powerful and effective. And the Living Water that flows freely between us brings even greater health and vitality.

At the time of this writing, I have the privilege of leading a team of people from our local church into the women's prison to minister to the inmates on a regular basis. We work as a team, each member sharing the responsibilities of teaching and leading. I was recently awarded "2024 Volunteer of the Year" for the work we do in the prison. As grateful as I am for the acknowledgement, I'm very much aware that I did not receive that award for my individual efforts. The team earned that award! And we cannot function well without each other. On any given ministry day at the prison, one reads Scripture, one leads worship, one prays, one teaches, and we all minister. We bring our gifts and use them together as a team with one goal—to lift up Jesus so others may see Him.

Our prison ministry team is a microcosm of the larger Body of Christ. We must function together to bring Jesus to people in a way that they can receive His love, grace, and forgiveness. Unfortunately, in the Body of Christ, we tend to function independently and lose the effectiveness and blessing of working together. Another way to describe this effectiveness and blessing of working together is to use the words unity and anointing. There is a supernatural anointing released when we function in unity. The New Living Translation uses the word harmony.

> *How wonderful and pleasant it is*
> *when brothers live together in harmony!*
> *For harmony is as precious as the anointing oil*
> *that was poured over Aaron's head,*
> *that ran down his beard*
> *and onto the border of his robe.*
> *Harmony is as refreshing as the dew from Mount Hermon*
> *that falls on the mountains of Zion.*
> *And there the* LORD *has pronounced his blessing,*
> *even life everlasting.* (Psalm 133)

The anointing oil was used in the ordination of the priests as they were prepared for service. Aaron was called by God and anointed to be the high priest of the Hebrew people. (See Leviticus 8). In the New Testament, Jesus became our ultimate High Priest, giving us the Holy Spirit as the anointing oil, preparing each of us to be ministering priests in the name of the one true God. We are one Body with one Head ministering with one Spirit, all under the authority of our one triune God.

And the anointing that is available to us and released through us as we walk in harmony with one another is powerful—not just for us today but for generations yet to come. As we see ourselves as part of the larger whole, we catch a glimpse of our generational influence. The prayers we pray today may reach fulfillment yet in the future. When we live our daily lives with eternity in mind, we're thinking generationally. What we do today affects tomorrow. How we conduct our lives today sets in motion blessings yet to be enjoyed or bondages to be overcome by future generations.

It's so easy to forget the ripple effect of our decisions as we live our daily lives. As a pebble is dropped into a body of water, consecutive rings emanate out from where the pebble entered the water. Our lives are like that pebble, and how we live creates emanating rings in our present and into the future.

So many of Israel's difficulties in Old Testament times occurred because God's people lived badly, affecting generations after them. Disregard for the effect of our sin on future generations is a sad outcome of our limited vision. Oh, that we would live with others in mind! Intergenerationally, we are still one Body.

My awareness of this concept of intergenerational responsibility has been heightened in the last few years as I have worked with my friends in Pakistan. Although the country of Pakistan is currently ninety-eight percent Muslim, the ministry we're doing is slowly, but assuredly changing that statistic.

We've thus far started two children's schools in which we are teaching children both academically and spiritually. These children are growing up with a Biblical—eternal—mindset. They're learning to be loved by Jesus Christ and to grow in that love toward others. We're also training women to sew, establishing sewing centers that teach the trade and teach the Word of God. As these women learn of Christ and grow in His Word, their families and communities begin to change. And the ministry team we've trained is evangelizing the surrounding area through open-air meetings, children's crusades, and Bible studies. The light of Jesus Christ is going forth to not only change those who are present but also those who are yet to be born. As the Gospel changes families, generations to come are transformed.

The Gospel message is a message about relationships—first with Christ and then with one another. It is one of community and interconnectedness, valuing others above self. *"For there is one body and one Spirit, just as you have been called to one glorious hope for the future. There is one Lord, one faith, one baptism, one God and Father of all, who is over all, in all, and living through all"* (Ephesians 4:4-6).

Chapter 3

AUTHORITY IN CHRIST

The Old Testament book of Haggai may seem like a strange place to begin talking about the authority given to us by the risen Christ, but there is a rich parallel between the people of Haggai's day—really every generation—and us today. For generations, the Old Testament prophets warned the Hebrew people that their idolatry and injustice would result in God's judgment. The people did not heed the prophets' warnings. In time, the northern kingdom of Israel was conquered by the Assyrian empire, and the southern kingdom of Judah was later conquered by the Babylonian empire.

After seventy years of captivity, the people of Judah were allowed to leave Babylon and return to their homeland. Their cities lay in ruins, and the once-beautiful Temple in the capital city of Jerusalem had been reduced to a pile of stones. As the people of Judah settled in, they began to rebuild their lives by constructing lovely homes for themselves. But the people seemed unconcerned about rebuilding the Temple—God's house. God sent the prophet Haggai to get their attention.

> *This is what the* Lord *of Heaven's Armies says: The people are saying, "The time has not yet come to rebuild the house of the* Lord*."*
>
> *Then the* Lord *sent this message through the prophet Haggai: "Why are you living in luxurious houses while my house lies in ruins? This is what the* Lord *of Heaven's Armies says: Look at what's happening to you! You have planted much but harvest little. You eat but are not satisfied. You drink but are still thirsty. You put on clothes but cannot keep warm. Your wages disappear as though you were putting them in pockets filled with holes!*
>
> *This is what the* Lord *of Heaven's Armies says: Look at what's happening to you! Now go up into the hills, bring down timber, and rebuild my house. Then I will take pleasure in it and be honored, says the* Lord*. You hoped for rich harvests, but they were poor. And when you brought your harvest home, I blew it away. Why? Because my house lies in ruins, says the* Lord *of Heaven's Armies, while all of you are busy building your own fine houses. It's because of you that the heavens withhold the dew and the earth produces no crops. I have called for a drought on your fields and hills—a drought to wither the grain and grapes and olive trees and all your other crops, a drought to starve you and your livestock and to ruin everything you have worked so hard to get."*
>
> (Haggai 1:2-11)

Because of the Hebrews' disobedience toward God, He allowed them to be taken captive by other nations. Their privileged position as His children was supposed to bring Light to the nations around them, but they misused their position and spent His blessings on themselves. Often, their idolatry didn't involve removing God completely; instead, they added other gods to their worship of the One true God. Either way, the result was the same—persistent disobedience brought judgment. Even after returning to Jerusalem from their captivity in Babylon, they still hadn't learned their lesson. They were distracted by building for themselves rather than building for God's Kingdom.

And here's where the concept of authority in Christ comes into our conversation. With every act of disobedience, the Israelites forfeited—at least temporarily—their authority to act on God's behalf to the people around them. The concept of authority is to act on another person's behalf with the power derived from that person's position. We, as Christians, are called to act on Christ's behalf to bring His power and rule to the people on Earth. When we live distracted lives, consumed by our own interests, we are erring in disobedience and forfeiting our rightful authority in Christ to shine brightly as His Light.

The New Testament letter to the Christians in Ephesus—written by the apostle Paul—gives us a look at the scope of power available to us by the authority of Christ:

> *I pray that your hearts will be flooded with light so that you can understand the confident hope he has given to those he called—his holy people who are his rich and glorious inheritance.*
>
> *I also pray that you will understand the incredible greatness of God's power for us who believe him. This is the same mighty power that raised Christ from the dead and seated him in the place of honor at God's right hand in the heavenly realms. Now he is far above any ruler or authority or power or leader or anything else—not only in this world but also in the world to come.* ***God has put all things under the***

> ***authority of Christ and has made him head over all things for the benefit of the church. And the church is his body; it is made full and complete by Christ, who fills all things everywhere with himself.***
>
> (Ephesians 1:18-23, emphasis mine)

Christ houses all the authority of heaven within himself, and the most amazing part of our relationship with Him is that He has delegated that authority to us! Matthew 28:18-20 says, *"Jesus came and told his disciples, 'I have been given all authority in heaven and on earth.* ***Therefore, go*** *and make disciples of all the nations, baptizing them in the name of the Father and the Son and the Holy Spirit. Teach these new disciples to obey all the commands I have given you. And be sure of this: I am with you always, even to the end of the age.'"* (Emphasis mine)

The word *therefore* in verse nineteen tends to evoke in us a sense of royal privilege; we enjoy the idea of Christ's authority being given to us. But we often neglect the word that follows—*go*! The authority given to us is not for us to feel good about ourselves or even to spend on ourselves. It is for the purpose of being the Light of Jesus Christ everywhere we go—to minister to people and permeate the atmosphere with the Gospel message. But we can't do that if we're focused on ourselves.

Christ's authority in our lives doesn't truly become activated until we are in an abiding relationship with Him. As Christians, we can tap into His authority on occasion with a surface-level relationship, but if we want to *live and function* in the full scope of His authority, we must truly abide in Him on an on-going basis. This was the grievous error the Israelites were making; they were living spiritually fractured lives rather than abiding in close relationship with God.

God's children were believing that they could go about living their own lives and simply add God in as a means of blessing—sort of like carrying around a lucky rabbit's foot. But God's Kingdom demands radical devotion from its followers. In the Kingdom of God, there is no room for spiritually fractured living. God was calling His children to wholehearted devotion. And today, He is still calling us to this devotion as well, which requires that we continually abide in Him. *He* is the power source of authority, and without Him, we have no authority.

Because we so easily drift into living spiritually fractured lives, you may be asking: What does an abiding relationship with Christ look like? An abiding relationship with Christ is a dedicated life fully surrendered to His rule and authority.

We often accept surface-level Christianity as normal, especially in the western world. But the term "surface-level Christianity" is really an oxymoron. When Christ calls us to follow Him, He's beckoning us into a radical commitment to follow His example. And God's Word—the Bible—is our map, our filter, and our plumb line. Allow me to explain each of these (map, filter, plumb line) using the analogy of a road trip.

If you set off on a trip to a place you've never visited and didn't have the benefit of GPS, you would need a map. I remember as a child and young adult taking trips across the country, driving to places I'd not yet been. There was no GPS at that time, so we would obtain a paper map of the state we were going to visit and a map of the entire United States to traverse the interstate highways. It was exciting to set off on our adventures! We plotted our route and carefully studied the maps as we went along to make sure we hadn't gotten off-course during our journey.

The Word of God—for the Christian—is our *map* for travelling through this life. I have heard Christians say that they only occasionally pick up the Word of God, or worse yet, they aren't really interested in reading it. There is absolutely no way to live the life God intends us to live without following His guidebook. That would be like setting off on a road trip without a map to guide you. You'll end up somewhere, but not likely where you thought you were going or where God intended. When we consider that our heavenly reward is based on living according to God's plans and intentions for our lives, it seems prudent that we pay close attention to His map.

His Word is not just our map, but also our *filter*. It's possible to set off on a carefully planned trip, execute the plan, and arrive at the destination without truly experiencing the journey. Life in Christ is not a series of boxes to be checked off. If we treat it that way, we'll miss the point of living. We need to be present and attentive to the Holy Spirit's interjections in our lives, and the Word of God trains us to be sensitive to Him. The Word of God—through the Holy Spirit—serves as our filter for decision-making, and it challenges us to examine our daily living.

Using our road trip analogy, one element of traveling that maps don't account for is weather. Let's say you were driving from California to Kentucky in the month of January. As you begin your trip, the weather may be chilly, but not disruptive. However, as you trek across the Rocky Mountains, you may have to adjust your plans. Being informed of weather forecasts and road conditions influences your decision-making. You would be foolish to continue your trip without filtering your travel plans through the current conditions. Likewise, we would be foolish to live our daily lives without the Holy Spirit-infused filter of God's Word.

Even if we successfully use the Word of God as our map and our Spirit-infused filter, we can still get bogged down along the journey. Back to our analogy… Let's imagine that we stop in a snowy, picturesque town in the Rocky Mountains to wait out the winter weather advisory. The town is comfortable and quaint, and we decide to stay a while longer which delays our journey indefinitely. There's nothing wrong with enjoying each day along the journey, but we need to be reminded that we've got further to travel, and we need to keep moving. Distractions—good and bad—in life can take our eyes off the goal and stall us out in our journeys. The Word of God serves not only as a map and a filter, but also as a *plumb line*, reminding us of what is important and where our focus needs to remain.

A plumb line is a tool used by contractors and masons to build walls that are perfectly straight, at a right angle to the earth. If a wall is built but isn't plumb, it is not secure and can easily be toppled. God's wisdom and standards of righteousness are clearly written for us in His Word, and they are our plumb line. But if we never read the Bible or treat it with disregard, we have nothing to measure our lives against. Then we tend to follow our desires rather than God's plans for our lives. When we don't use the plumb line of the Word of God, we won't even know that we are walking a crooked path headed for disaster.

So, how does this tie in with walking in the authority given to us by Jesus? The fullness of Christ's authority becomes more and more accessible to us as we align our lives with God's design. He is the Holy One—without sin and absolutely right in everything He does. His standards do not change. We are the ones who must align to His holy standards. And then, His life-giving authority can flow through our lives to affect the people around us.

The Hebrew children in Haggai's day realized that they had fallen away from God's plan and standards. God arrested their attention and challenged them to think carefully about the direction they were headed. *"Now therefore, thus says the* Lord *of hosts: 'Consider your ways!'"* (Haggai 1:5, NKJV). Commentator David Guzik says, "The Hebrew figure of speech for this phrase is literally 'put your heart on your roads'" (Blue Letter Bible, Study Guide for Haggai 1). God was telling them to exchange their apathetic approach to His ways with heart-felt devotion. God asks us as well to consider the direction of our lives and determine if we need to change the trajectory of our path.

The people of Judah repented of their distractions and unrighteousness and got to work building the Temple. And then God said, *"I am giving you a promise now while the seed is still in the barn... from this day onward I will bless you"* (Haggai 2:19). Their blessed lives were then meant to be a witness to the nations around them, exclaiming that God is the Holy One of Israel who pours himself—His authority and blessing—out on those who align their hearts with His.

If we want to walk in the authority available to us by Christ, we must intentionally pursue an abiding relationship with Him. And we'll find that as our authority in Christ is activated to a greater degree, we will begin to experience the powerful spiritual gifts in action—which we'll discuss in Chapter 4.

Chapter 4

SPIRITUAL GIFTS

There is a growing hunger inside me to see people healed and set free—mentally, physically, spiritually, and emotionally. My passionate desire is due in part to the pain I see inflicted on the lives of people I love. But it's mostly due to reading the Word of God and seeing what could be—or perhaps what should be. Jesus' words in the pages of Scripture echo in my heart and mind, reminding me that the Kingdom of heaven has come among us: "*The Spirit of the* Lord *is upon me, for he has anointed me to bring Good News to the poor. He has sent me to proclaim that captives will be released, that the blind will see, that the oppressed will be set free, and that the time of the* Lord*'s favor has come*" (Luke 4:18-19).

These words were first uttered by the prophet Isaiah when he was foretelling of the Messiah and His commissioning.

> *The Spirit of the Sovereign* Lord *is upon me, for the* Lord *has anointed me to bring good news to the poor. He has sent me to comfort the brokenhearted and to proclaim that captives will be released and prisoners will be freed. He has sent me to tell*

those who mourn that the time of the LORD's favor has come, and with it, the day of God's anger against their enemies.
(Isaiah 61:1-2)

Although Isaiah's prophetic commissioning was attributed to the Christ approximately 700 years before His birth and ministry, Jesus clearly fulfilled His commission while on Earth and then charged us—His Church—with the same task.

After Jesus had been crucified and resurrected, He appeared many times to His closest disciples. In His last appearance to them, He said:

"Go into all the world and preach the Good News to everyone. Anyone who believes and is baptized will be saved. But anyone who refuses to believe will be condemned. These miraculous signs will accompany those who believe: They will cast out demons in my name, and they will speak in new languages. They will be able to handle snakes with safety, and if they drink anything poisonous, it won't hurt them. They will be able to place their hands on the sick, and they will be healed" (Mark 16:15-18)

The New Testament writer Mark records that

When the Lord Jesus had finished talking with them, he was taken up into heaven and sat down in the place of honor at God's right hand. And the disciples went everywhere and preached, and the Lord worked through them, confirming what they said by many miraculous signs.
(Mark 16:19-20)

Jesus' disciples had walked with Him for three years and watched Him minister love, grace, mercy, and power to the people around them. Jesus had also confronted wrong motives and dealt with self-righteousness in leaders who were supposed to be leading others in love and Spirit-filled power. So, the disciples had been given the perfect example—a living illustration of the Spirit-filled Christian life. And Jesus reminded His disciples that they needed the empowerment of the Holy Spirit to live the kind of life He had lived on Earth.

> *During the forty days after he suffered and died, he appeared to the apostles from time to time, and he proved to them in many ways that he was actually alive. And he talked to them about the Kingdom of God.*
>
> *Once when he was eating with them, he commanded them, "Do not leave Jerusalem until the Father sends you the gift he promised, as I told you before. John baptized with water, but in just a few days you will be baptized with the Holy Spirit."*
>
> (Acts 1:3-5)

There is absolutely no way the disciples could have carried out the monumental task of witnessing, disciple-making, and being a conduit of God's power without the empowerment of the Holy Spirit. And neither can we. But with that empowerment, God reminds us that anything is possible. Through His Holy Spirit, we function in the same powerful anointing as our Messiah. "*The Spirit of God, who raised Jesus from the dead, lives in you*" (Romans 8:11a). And that same Holy Spirit imparts to us spiritual gifts which enable us to carry out Christ's command.

God's spiritual gifts in our lives can be categorized into three subsets: ministry gifts, manifestation gifts, and motivational gifts. We can look to Ephesians 4, 1 Corinthians 12, and Romans 12 as representative lists of the many gifts. In the ministry gifts listed in Ephesians 4:11-16, we see gifts such as apostles, prophets, evangelists, pastors, teachers. In 1 Corinthians 12:4-31, we see manifestation gifts such as healing, miracles, discernment, tongues, wisdom, word of knowledge, and great faith. And listed in Romans 12:6-10, the seven motivational gifts include prophecy, serving, teaching, exhortation, giving, leading, and mercy.

As wonderful as all these gifts are, they are completely useless if they are not borne out of love for others. And that love is not manufactured in our human hearts. The closer we walk with Jesus—the more we abide in Him—the more effectively we become a conduit of His love and His gifts. And He is the only Source of true love and effective ministry.

The concept of an abiding relationship with Christ is so easily overlooked in our fast-paced, achievement/goal-oriented society. Let me illustrate abiding in Christ using the concept of marriage. In a marriage, two people can be legally married but not have a relationship in which they abide with one another. They may live in the same house, attend the same church, and name the same family members as their own, but if they don't intentionally create an ongoing loving bond between them, they're not truly abiding with one another. They are simply doing life alongside each other.

We have the tendency to treat our relationship with Christ the same way. We *check all the boxes* in our relationship with Christ but do not intentionally participate in closely abiding. To abide is to dwell with another—to intentionally live in deep relationship with them. And that requires actively giving and receiving love. God himself *is* love. So, when we abide in Him, we actively participate in receiving His love and giving it away to others.

The apostle Paul reminds us just how important this God-love is:

> *If I could speak all the languages of earth and of angels, but didn't love others, I would only be a noisy gong or a clanging cymbal. If I had the gift of prophecy, and if I understood all of God's secret plans and possessed all knowledge, and if I had such faith that I could move mountains, but didn't love others, I would be nothing. If I gave everything I have to the poor and even sacrificed my body, I could boast about it; but if I didn't love others, I would have gained nothing.*
>
> (1 Corinthians 13:1-3)

Paul goes on to describe what true love looks like in the next few verses.

> *Love is patient and kind. Love is not jealous or boastful or proud or rude. It does not demand its own way. It is not irritable, and it keeps no record of being wronged. It does not rejoice about injustice but rejoices whenever the truth wins out. Love never gives up, never loses faith, is always hopeful, and endures through every circumstance.*
>
> (1 Corinthians 13:4-7)

We so often quote verses four through seven in this chapter during wedding ceremonies or on Valentine's Day, but the love between a man and a woman is only a small part of the overall purpose of the apostle Paul's words. Verses four through seven give us a picture of the kind of love we're commissioned to give to others. There is no way for us to carry out loving others in this manner without abiding in Christ.

Let's briefly look at the chapters surrounding 1 Corinthians 13 to put these verses in the larger context of Paul's letter to the people of Corinth. Chapter eleven of 1 Corinthians discusses elevating others above ourselves in corporate worship gatherings so that we are concerned for the whole, not focused on ourselves. Chapter twelve—as we saw earlier—discusses spiritual gifts. And chapter fourteen laser-focuses on the gifts of tongues and prophecy mostly in the corporate worship setting. So, chapter thirteen is nestled right in the middle of Paul's letter, emphasizing corporate worship gatherings and challenging readers to be governed by love. Yes, spouses should love one another according to chapter thirteen verses four through seven, but context beckons us to apply the virtue of love to the whole of our lives, particularly as we minister to others in our churches and in our communities.

Within the local church, we tend to apply the concepts of positions and titles in the way that the world uses them. With our natural minds, we might see the position of Lead Pastor as a coveted position of power and authority. Or perhaps we see a staff position as something to be achieved. Maybe we look at someone who functions in the gift of healing or prophecy and wish that was us. But Jesus was never concerned about title or position, and yet He is the ultimate Healer, the forever High Priest, the King of Kings, and the truest voice of prophecy. Our primary objective should simply be to draw near to Jesus and allow His love to transform us. When we are changed, we operate out of His endless well of love, and we are not concerned about position or title. Spiritual gifts then flow through us as He desires.

As God transforms us, our eyes are opened to the people around us—to the hurting, the joyful, the needy. We truly notice others. We look deeply into their lives, concerned more about them than about the gifts or positions that might entice us. Everything we do in the Kingdom of God must be governed by *His love* coursing through us, which brings powerful transformation in others' lives. As much as we want to believe that we can effect change through our own effort or through spiritual gifting, the only change that lasts comes through love—His love.

"Three things will last forever—faith, hope, and love—and the greatest of these is love" (1 Corinthians 13:13). One thing matters most… *"the greatest of these is love."*

Chapter 5

PERSONAL GROWTH

As we draw nearer to Christ, spend time in His Word, and give Him access to our hearts, we realize that we're beginning to grow—to mature. The term personal growth is a broad term—one we use to describe a combination of physical, spiritual, mental, and emotional progress. And growth in all those areas is certainly necessary for our overall health. But one aspect of personal growth that we don't often acknowledge is growth through limitations.

I am naturally a type-A personality with a high capacity for administrating several things at one time, and I see most every significant need I encounter as an opportunity to lead the charge in fulfilling that need. It's usually out of a love for starting new things, seeing new possibilities come to life, and improving things that need a touch of excellence. I could see myself doing all kinds of things like pastoring a church, building a dream center, administrating a school, starting new ministries, or leading a large company, and the list goes on and on. I love learning, and I would enjoy obtaining my next college degree while accomplishing all the things listed above. Are you exhausted from reading my extensive list? Although thinking about achieving all those things energizes me, God has placed limits on my life for my own good.

When I use the word limits, I cringe a little bit. Perhaps you do, too. My natural inclination is to break through limits and push forward with drive and determination. Limits are meant to be broken—or so I thought. But God has invited me to look at limits differently. They aren't all meant to be broken through. Some limits serve as a beautiful gift to keep our lives from spinning out of control.

Much like a controlled fire that breaks through the firewall meant to contain it and consequently does enormous damage, our lives can quickly spin out of control when we challenge our God-induced limits. I am learning to appreciate God's *firewalls* in my life.

It seems that one benefit to God's limits on my life is to help me be attentive to what's happening in my present. Otherwise, I would always be living in *what comes next*. And I would lose my deep longing to spend unhurried time with the Lord.

As each person gets to know themselves—their spiritual gifts and their own limits—they become aware of signals that indicate a breach of those limits. In my life, I begin to feel overwhelmed by my long list of things to do, and I start *trading people for tasks*. My vision then breaks away from the importance of people in the present and drifts to the tasks that will bring me forward movement in one or more areas of my life. Another warning sign that I have taken on too much is that I'm *distracted* during my morning time with Jesus. Through these signals, I know when God is trying to tell me I'm becoming overloaded, and it's my job to heed His warnings.

Several years ago, I had an encounter with the Lord that forever altered my view of God's limits for me. One day, I asked God who I would be without Him. That may seem like an unusual question to ask God, but I'm guessing His Holy Spirit placed the thought in my mind. What He showed me radically shifted the way I think about my life. He gave me a vision —a mental video—of an artist painting a portrait. I was the subject of the portrait, and the canvas was turned away from me during the painting process. I was not allowed to see it until it was complete. When the artist was finished, I was quite curious as he turned the canvas so I could see his work.

I think our natural assumption in answering the question "God, who would I be without You?" would be a person who is homeless, destitute, penniless, and alone. So, I was quite shocked by what I saw on the artist's canvas. It wasn't at all what I expected.

The image of me without God wasn't destitute—it was quite the opposite. In the portrait, I was a successful CEO, well-dressed, attractive, and wealthy. I wasn't alone; I instinctively knew that I had people all around me, working diligently for a company to which they felt loyal. You may be thinking, "So, what's the problem with that?" The moment the artist turned the canvas to face me, I was staring into the eyes of a woman who had everything but didn't know love. Her eyes were hollow, lacking the life-giving light of Christ. And I instinctively knew that although she was surrounded by people who tried to love her, she had no capacity to receive that love.

I'm still moved to tears as I recount that vision because it so imprinted on my spirit my desperate need for the love of my Savior. Without His love, this life and all its trappings are meaningless. And without His love, I wouldn't know how to receive love from others. To be known and loved by Christ is our highest privilege—our most valuable purpose—to which we could ever aspire. And since the day God gave me that vision, its clear message has informed many of my decisions.

Each day, my priority is time with Jesus. It's the first thing I do—just being with Him. I read His Word and ask Him to speak to my heart. I bask in His love for me and allow His Word to challenge me. As opportunities in life come my way, I weigh them against my ability to maintain my personal time with Jesus. If a new responsibility will potentially cut into my time with the Lord, I either relinquish the responsibility or adjust it to make room for my most important work of the day.

I have avoided pursuing jobs, positions, or titles that would entice me away from my time with Him. I have chosen to accept what He brings me because He knows what is best for me. If left to myself, I would run at a pace of achievement that would leave everyone around me in the dust of my wake. But that's the woman in the painting. And I don't want that life. I want to live in the pace of basking in His love and in the joy of relationship with others. That may not be a very popular approach to life, but *I have seen* what I would be without His moment-by-moment presence in my life, and I wholeheartedly choose an abiding life with my Savior.

As I allow Him to govern my life—my time, my personality, my decisions—I've found that I live with a much greater impact for His Kingdom. Peace, joy, and love become the hallmark of my life, and people respond to His presence in me. Most people like what's produced in the life of a person who has submitted themselves fully to the will and pace of the Master. They respond. However, becoming that person who is fully submitted is quite challenging.

This kind of life requires intentionality and sacrifice—the willingness to live within the limits God places on us. Think about the limits of our state and federal laws. They are intended to protect us and others around us. When we choose to live beyond those limits, we threaten our own well-being and the well-being of others. Punishment is exacted to curb our law-defying actions. The laws themselves are limits, and the punishment that ensues is also a limit. When we learn to function within the laws of our land, we experience freedom that avoids punishment. We'll talk more about freedom in a subsequent chapter. But until we learn to see God's limits in our lives as a gift, we're stunting our own personal growth and diminishing our effectiveness for His Kingdom.

Our unwillingness to live within God's limits affects the people around us. For instance, we may see the need to start a ministry in our local church, and if we jump in to start it when it's not our God-assigned task, we're robbing our brothers and sisters in Christ from *their God-given opportunity*. Or we could be operating outside of God's timing. If we initiate something before God's timing, we may be putting undue strain on others. One example in scripture of living within God's limits is when God told King David that he was not the one to build His temple.

> *David summoned all the officials of Israel to Jerusalem—the leaders of the tribes, the commanders of the army divisions, the other generals and captains, the overseers of the royal property and livestock, the palace officials, the mighty men, and all the other brave warriors in the kingdom. David rose to his feet and said, "My brothers and my people! It was my desire to build a Temple where the Ark of the LORD's Covenant, God's footstool, could rest permanently. I made the necessary preparations for building it, but God said to me, 'You must not build a Temple to honor my name, for you are a warrior and have shed much blood...' He said to me, 'Your*

> *son Solomon will build my Temple and its courtyards, for I have chosen him as my son, and I will be his father.'"*
>
> (1 Chronicles 28:1-3, 6)

Honestly, that's a difficult story for me to read. David saw a God-glorifying need—to build a house for the Lord among His people. And even though King David was positioned to complete the task and had all the resources needed to do the job, God said no. God had chosen David's son Solomon to build the Temple, and it wasn't time to begin building. David accepted God's decision, and he chose to help prepare for the future. As David waited for Solomon's ascent to the throne, he amassed the needed materials for Solomon to build the Temple. David used God's limitation on his own life to prepare for the next generation's success.

A two-fold question for us to consider is, "What is God asking me to do, and who is God asking me to support?" If you have the desire to see a need met, you may or may not be the one to meet it. However, even if you aren't the architect for the project, you can support the one who is. And don't forget to consider if now is the right time. All these considerations are part of living a life led by the Spirit of God. We must listen to Him with the intent to obey. To live any other way is to disrespect our God-given limits.

You may be thinking, "I'm not the go-getter type. So, I'm comfortable with not pushing forward. I don't have a problem with respecting God's limits." Perhaps God is drawing you forward to break through your *self-imposed limitations*. If we are living in our own self-imposed limitations, we may be holding back out of fear of the unknown or the disruption of our comfort zone.

The ability to risk trading what we currently have for what *could be* requires trust. And in the lives of Christians, that trust must be in God's ability to lead us. It's admittedly easier to protect the status quo and stay within the limits we've placed on ourselves. Job changes, start-ups, establishing (or re-establishing) relationships, positional adjustments, etc. are all risk-taking activities. But if God is challenging us to take those risks, then it's imperative that we respond in obedience.

Living within our comfort zone and protecting the status quo often leads to a life of stunted growth. When we refuse to trust God's leading in our lives, we halt our growth process. Our lives become an exercise in self-protection rather than an adventure in trust.

Our natural inclination is to either push past God-given restraints in our lives or hold back when He desires that we move forward. Either way, God is inviting us to willingly choose to live within *His* gift of limits. He has given us just one life to live for Him. And our intentional obedience to live within His limits is crucial to our participation in the work of His Kingdom.

Chapter 6

FREEDOM

As we pay attention to the Holy Spirit's leading in our lives and learn to operate within His limits, we experience true freedom. The world around us would argue that freedom comes from throwing off limits and pursuing our own dreams by our own methods. Even as Christians, when we choose to live our own way, we're living at odds with God, and that brings bondage, not freedom. True freedom comes from walking in God's ways (according to His Word) and in His timing. His Word is our lifeline to walking in freedom. The psalmist wrote:

> *Do not snatch your word of truth from me, for your regulations are my only hope. I will keep on obeying your instructions forever and ever. I will walk in freedom, for I have devoted myself to your commandments.*
>
> (Psalm 119:43-45)

Our devotion—our obedience—to God's Word demonstrates our love for God. It's easy to view obedience to His Word as cumbersome and limiting, but the opposite is true. The closer we adhere to God's ways, the greater freedom we experience. As we experience this godly freedom, we find ourselves walking in greater love toward people.

Saint Augustine was a philosopher and theologian in the fourth century. In his writings, he said that sin is a lack of love—either for God or for the people around you. Long before Augustine, the apostle Paul reminded us of this as well.

> *For you have been called to live in freedom, my brothers and sisters. But don't use your freedom to satisfy your sinful nature. Instead, use your freedom to serve one another in love.* (Galatians 5:13)

Our responsibility as Christians is to keep our love for God and for one another at the forefront of our minds, guiding our thinking, our decisions, and our actions. Saint Augustine is famously quoted saying that "The essence of sin is disordered love." When we love *less-important things* more and *more-important things* less, we are living with disordered loves. So, living with Biblical priorities is key to our sense of freedom, which is ultimately expressed in our love for others.

James, the half-brother of Jesus and the leader of the Jerusalem church, writes a compelling argument for our right prioritization of love in chapter one of his letter to Jewish believers:

> *So get rid of all the filth and evil in your lives, and humbly accept the word God has planted in your hearts, for it has the power to save your souls.* (James 1:21)

When we examine the phrase "to save your souls," we see that the word *save* in this verse is from the Greek word *sozo* meaning to deliver, protect, heal, and be made whole. Our true freedom—freedom from all that would not benefit us—comes from applying the Word of God in our lives. Freedom comes from accepting what Christ did for us and devoting our lives to follow His ways. The apostle Paul said it this way, *"He (God) is so rich in kindness and grace that he purchased our freedom with the blood of his Son and forgave our sins"* (Ephesians 1:7).

No greater sacrifice has ever been made to grant us freedom. The Son of God left heaven, became human flesh, was beaten, died an excruciating death, and was raised to life again to grant us freedom. Oh, what kindness and generosity! To scorn His gift toward us by living our own way is the height of ingratitude. And the Bible poses some incredibly negative consequences to a life lived without God's guidance:

"And since they did not see fit to acknowledge God, God gave them up to a debased mind to do what ought not to be done" (Romans 1:28, ESV). That's bondage! In contrast, freedom says:

> *But if you look carefully into* ***the perfect law that sets you free****, and if you do what it says and don't forget what you heard, then God will bless you for doing it.*
>
> (James 1:25, emphasis mine)

Christian freedom must never be viewed as the liberty to violate Christ's commands. It is the power to obey them" (Fire Bible Life Publishers, p.2171). Dying to our own desires and submitting to Christ's commands may seem like the hardest thing in the world to do, but those who have intentionally chosen to live within His guidelines have tasted true freedom. *"For the Lord is the Spirit, and wherever the Spirit of the Lord is, there is freedom"* (2 Corinthians 3:17).

Because God is himself creative and wise, we experience greater and greater freedom as we tap into His wealth of unlimited potential when we choose to live His way. It's sad to watch incredibly intelligent people live without godly wisdom.

Their lives are on a destructive path that will eventually result in self-absorption.

But God has given us the potential to live with incredible possibility as we abide in Him. A.W. Tozer wrote, "The widest thing in the universe is not space; it is the potential capacity of the human heart. Being made in the image of God, it is capable of almost unlimited extension in all directions. And one of the world's greatest tragedies is that we allow our hearts to shrink until there is room in them for little besides ourselves" (*The Root of the Righteous,* 1955).

We, as Christians, have the tendency to equate freedom with only our salvation. Yes, that is the most critical decision to release us from bondage and initiate our freedom. But our freedom doesn't stop there; it begins there. God's desire is to bring exponential Kingdom growth through our lives. We mature as He grows His Kingdom through us.

Decades ago, I began an experiment with God. I had come to trust Him implicitly, and I wondered what my life would look like if I just kept saying yes to God. So, when I sensed the prompting of His Holy Spirit, I would simply say yes to His leadership. My life has become an adventure with God that is both challenging and incredibly satisfying. Freedom in Christ has given me the ability to adventure with Him, growing both in personal capacity and Kingdom multiplication. I'll share an example from my life of how saying yes to God brings unlimited potential.

The story begins with an act of obedience—a seed planted—nearly twenty-five years ago from the time of this writing. I'm sure the story actually has its roots long before that, but we'll pick up my part of the story from twenty-five years ago. Our children were very young, and we had begun the journey of educating our kids. Being an educator by profession, I took my own children's education very seriously. And my personal conviction was to raise them in an environment where God was welcome. At times that meant private Christian education, and at other times, that meant periods of homeschooling. Either way, their education was never free; it was costly.

At a church event one day, the Good Samaritan Baptist Mission was offering us the opportunity to sponsor a child to go to school. For about $30 each month, a child who would otherwise not have the opportunity could go to school. The Holy Spirit spoke to my heart, "If you'll make sure one of these children has a Christian education, I'll make sure your children do, too." At that point in our lives, with three young children, $30 a month felt like a sacrifice. But God had made me a promise, and I was all in!

Our child from Nicaragua was named Juan, and his picture hung on our refrigerator for 14 years as we sponsored him all the way through his education. We lovingly called him the brother that our son Jonathon never had, as they were one year apart in age. We rejoiced the day Juan graduated from high school, and eventually his picture came down from our refrigerator. Our kids have many memories of prayers prayed for Juan and his family over those years. And our kids knew the story of God's promise—that their Christ-centered education would be taken care of because we obediently provided for Juan's Christ-centered education. God did exactly what He said He would do. That part of the story ended about ten years ago when Juan and the last of our three children graduated from high school, but God has a funny way of working behind the scenes when we're not aware of it.

In recent years, God has blessed me with fifteen books to publish. He has entrusted us with a beautiful ministry in Pakistan. And He has added many ministry partners for whom we are eternally grateful. But God most certainly isn't finished.

Not long ago, I received a message through social media that asked, "Did you sponsor a child in Nicaragua? I am Juan." Absolutely overjoyed to hear from him, we began conversing about what he was currently doing. At that time, he said he was preparing to graduate in December from a seminary in south Texas. God has called him to be a church planter, and he said he will go wherever God sends him to plant churches and make disciples.

Tears flowed down my cheeks as I realized what God had started from that one act of obedience twenty-five years ago. What God gave me as a promise to educate our own children turned into the beginning of exponential Kingdom multiplication. As of this writing, God has given us over 350 children—in two schools—in Pakistan to educate who will take the gospel out further and to generations yet to come. And who knows how many lives will be changed through Juan's church planting? In addition, we have over one hundred ministry partners who invest in the Kingdom work. Their simple acts of obedience to God's leading in their own lives are also changing the world.

Henri Nouwen said, "God's kingdom is the place of abundance where every generous act overflows its original bounds and becomes part of the unbounded grace of God at work in the world" (*The Spirituality of Fundraising*, p.46). Now *that* sounds like freedom! God is truly the magnificent One who has forgiven us of our sins and freed us from our disordered love.

Chapter 7

SUFFERING

As we enjoy walking in the freedom purchased for us by Christ, it doesn't take long for us to realize that this life is just as full of suffering as it is joy. We often view joy and suffering as opposites—one we willingly embrace and the other we vigorously push away.

But God instructs us to participate in both joy and suffering in this life:

> *Dear friends, don't be surprised at the fiery trials you are going through, as if something strange were happening to you. Instead, be very glad—for these trials make you partners with Christ in his* ***suffering****, so that you will have the wonderful* ***joy*** *of seeing his glory when it is revealed to all the world.*
>
> (1 Peter 4:12-13, emphasis mine)

Upon reading those verses, I'm reminded of the suffering many of our brothers and sisters in Christ around the world endure at the hands of persecutors. The nonprofit organization that I founded works with a local pastor and a team of ministers in Pakistan to educate children and empower women in villages of extreme poverty. Pakistan is a country in which ninety-eight percent of the population practices Islam, and many of these Muslim believers live at odds with their Christian neighbors. The mere suggestion that a Christian would disrespect the Quran can ignite extreme violence. We see persecution applied in the lives of these Christians far too often.

Within the last month (at the time of this writing), two hundred Christian homes and twenty-two churches were burned in the Pakistani town of Jaranwala, leaving families with no homes, no belongings, and no food. This persecution is indeed suffering—a form of suffering with which most Christians in the western world are unfamiliar.

But suffering is much broader than persecution. The suffering of a grieving spouse or parent is indeed heartbreaking. The suffering of an accident victim whose life is devastatingly altered reminds us that this life brings unwanted difficulty. In most cases, we wouldn't choose to suffer willingly, but there must be an understanding on our part that some degree of suffering will invade our lives. It's hard for us to imagine that suffering could bring any good to our lives, but God views suffering differently than we do.

Suffering and joy—according to God—are beautifully intertwined. Both are needful for us in this life as we learn to draw nearer to Him. But we're not left to endure suffering on our own. God is ever-present in both our celebrations and in our sorrows. His Word is replete with examples of real people living a real human experience.

The Old Testament book of Psalms contains expressions of celebratory joy and deep sorrow. It would be much more satisfying to read the joyful psalms, expecting that to be our total life's reality. But God knew we would encounter just as much suffering as joy and that we would need the comfort of those who have walked sorrowful paths before us. The psalmists give us a view of suffering that assists us in seeing it from God's perspective.

Many of the psalms recorded in the Old Testament are laments—passionate expressions of grief and suffering. For instance, Psalm 13 was written by David:

O LORD, how long will you forget me? Forever?
How long will you look the other way?
How long must I struggle with anguish in my soul,
with sorrow in my heart every day?
How long will my enemy have the upper hand?
Turn and answer me, O LORD *my God!*
Restore the sparkle to my eyes, or I will die.
Don't let my enemies gloat, saying, 'We have defeated him!'
Don't let them rejoice at my downfall.
But I trust in your unfailing love.
I will rejoice because you have rescued me.
I will sing to the LORD
Because he is good to me.

This psalm is a clear expression of David's intense suffering and his on-going confusion. And David had a lot to lament during his life. He was belittled by his brothers and disregarded by his father. The reigning king that David worked for and esteemed tried to kill him—more than once! The promises God made to David seemed faraway and impossible to obtain. When God finally fulfilled His promise to David and made him king of Israel, enemy nations tried to conquer and oppress his people. David buried some of his own children. And David's son Absolom conspired to usurp David's role as king.

David suffered many difficult things during his lifetime, but in each situation, he wasn't afraid to tell God what he felt. David spoke honestly with God about what he was going through.

David began Psalm 13 by asking God how long He'd be absent from David's situation. We all can empathize with David's emotional state. Although God has promised that He'll never leave us nor forsake us, our emotions tell us quite the opposite when we're experiencing intense situations. Deep pain clouds our vision. Fear creeps into our minds. Our imaginations run wild. And *then we worry* about all the terrifying outcomes we've imagined. We begin to wonder where God is in all our suffering. The beautiful—but often forgotten—truth is that He's been with us all along, inviting us to find refuge in His presence.

In the psalm, David moves from searching for God's presence to asking God how long this confusing in-between season will last. When we're experiencing intense suffering, life feels dark and upside down, and we don't know how to make the pain stop. We just want the suffering to end—or at least know that it has a timestamp. One of the hardest parts of waiting in the in-between season is not knowing when it will end.

The desperation we feel drives us to look for solutions to our pain-filled circumstances. And it's in that in-between season when we are most vulnerable to developing unhealthy habits, addictions, and dangerous relationships. Everything inside of us wants to break free from the gnawing pain, and we'll do just about anything to numb our distress. But God is inviting us to find consolation and peace in His presence rather than pursue empty substitutions that cannot satisfy.

In the Old Testament book of Jeremiah, God challenged the people of Judah to stop looking to pleasures outside His presence to satisfy their deep longings. "'*...my people have exchanged their* *glorious God for worthless idols! The heavens are shocked at such a thing and shrink back in horror and dismay,' says the* LORD. *'For my people have done two evil things: They have abandoned me—the fountain of living water. And they have dug for themselves cracked cisterns that can hold no water at all!'"* (Jeremiah 2:11b-13).

We so easily do the same thing when we are in the middle of suffering. We try to find relief from our distress through medication, addictions, unhealthy relationships, and isolation. But it doesn't have to be that way. Although it's not easy, it's very possible to submit our feelings of desperation to God and willingly sit in the pain while He processes our healing and our growth. We must trust that, at the right time, He will bring us out of our pain.

And the time of waiting in the in-between season is not wasted time when we yield to God's processes in our lives. God uses that in-between time to do a deep work in us. If we allow Him access to the deepest places in our hearts, He strips us of our self-reliance and frees us from unhealthy attachments—physically, emotionally, and relationally. During those difficult days of waiting, submission, and healing, we desperately need the nearness and comfort of the Holy Spirit. He is the powerful help we need as we navigate our pain in the long darkness.

We see in Psalm 13 that once David has expressed his difficulty in waiting for God's intervention, he moves on, asking God to shield him from the onslaught of enemies—real or perceived. During our waiting in the in-between season—when we are most vulnerable—we often feel as if we're being attacked from all sides. That feeling is not entirely unfounded.

Sometimes it's the actions of others that landed us in our distress. We're wounded at the hand of another—sometimes at the hand of a close friend or relative. That betrayal can feel overwhelmingly painful. And once we're in that place of vulnerability, it's as if we are easy prey to people who would like to see us fall.

The true enemy of our souls is happy to employ willing people to harm us and add insult to injury. We desperately need to be rescued from the onslaught of evil against us. Our rescue comes from what David said next. *"But I trust in your unfailing love."* Abiding in God's presence and immersing ourselves in His Word causes us—over time—to develop a deep trust in the faithful love of God. He is our One true answer and our sure source of help.

But I trust in your unfailing love.
I will rejoice because you have rescued me.
I will sing to the Lord
Because he is good to me.

This perspective shift requires us to take our eyes off the source of our pain and direct our gaze toward the Lord. When David wrote the end of Psalm 13, nothing externally had changed. He was still in a desperate situation. He was still waiting, and his enemies were still pursuing him. But his spirit had found peace in God's presence. And then joy erupted within him as he praised God in the middle of his difficulty.

When we are experiencing intense suffering, it's crucial for us to remember that although our feelings are very real —and God-given—we cannot allow our feelings to dictate our decisions and actions. We must be aware that we were created as a spirit-being made in God's image who has been gifted with a mind, will, and emotions and lives in a physical body. That means our God-infused spirit should be in control of our decisions and actions. We should not allow ourselves to be ruled by our intellect, emotions, or flesh.

To be ruled by the intellect is to assign reason or outcome to our problems and enact our own solutions rather than relying on God to lead us through. To be ruled by our emotions is to choose to exalt our pain, confusion, depression, or anger over quieting ourselves before the Lord. To be ruled by our flesh is to reach for whatever will numb the pain we feel internally—no matter the cost.

When we allow our spirit-man to be in control, we've positioned ourselves to receive God's answers to our difficulties. It's important that we choose to rejoice in the goodness of God even before our external circumstances change. And we can't put God on a timeline. We don't get to choose when our circumstances will shift. But God is inviting us to choose Him in our waiting.

We tend to equate our sense of joy with the correct alignment of our circumstances, but joy exists both inside and outside the confines of our circumstances. And whether we believe it or not, suffering isn't our enemy; it's often our invitation to experience God more deeply.

Our tendency is to fully feel joy and fully repel suffering. But God wants us to bear both well because there is richness in both. Our greatest challenge is often to simply remember that God is present in both our joy and our suffering.

Chapter 8

HIS GRACE DISPLAYED

After we have endured a particularly trying season of suffering, we are tempted to press forward and never look back. But that response conveys an attitude that somehow the suffering we experienced was wasted time in our lives—all too gladly forgotten. With God, nothing we go through is wasted. And if we allow the past to inform our present and our future, we'll find that His grace—especially experienced during seasons of suffering—is more evident in our lives than ever.

I had an experience many years ago that still influences my thinking today. I told the story in the book I wrote, *Trophies of His Grace* (published by Dream Releaser Publishing), and I'll recount it here.

In my early teen years, I was a competitive gymnast. I truly loved gymnastics and spent as many hours a week as I could at the gym. Overall, participating in gymnastics was a wonderful experience in my life, but there was a brief period of time when I allowed it to become an unhealthy obsession. During that time, I allowed gymnastics to consume my thoughts and actions.

Everything I did was focused on the purpose of becoming a better gymnast.

I began to choose my food carefully, weighing out in my mind which foods would perfect my body's ability to perform. I looked at myself in the mirror for the purpose of honing my physical body for efficiency and effectiveness in winning competitions. And before long, I fell prey to the cycle of anorexia nervosa.

When I looked at myself in the mirror, I saw an overweight young gymnast. I would step on the scale and plan how I could make the numbers on the scale go down by the next day. I was practicing in the gym more and more hours each week, and I was eating less and less food. I couldn't see what I was doing to myself.

The image I saw in the mirror day after day never changed, although the descending numbers on the scale were rewarding my efforts in limiting my eating.

Finally, after several weeks of this anorexic cycle, my mother said to me one day, "Debbie, if you don't stop losing weight, I'll have to take you out of gymnastics."

By speaking those words, my mother became my enemy. In my distorted thinking, I convinced myself that she simply wanted to prevent me from reaching my potential. I still couldn't see myself properly in the mirror, so her threat seemed to me to be completely unfounded.

Then one day as I rounded the corner into my mother's bedroom with the long, mirrored closets, I caught a glimpse of myself in the mirror. And for the first time in two months, I saw my body as it really was—an unhealthy, skeletal-like frame. The sight horrified me.

Then as I stood there frightened by what I saw, my eyes observed my image in the mirror shift back to the overweight body I had been seeing all along. At that moment, I realized my mind was believing a lie. I knew I needed help. I knew my mother had been right all along. I ran to her and told her what I had seen in the mirror, and in time, my mother led me back to a healthy weight.

Mom told me later that she and my doctor had decided to admit me to the local hospital if a significant change did not take place almost immediately. Then they prayed together and asked God to open my eyes. They received the answer to their prayers that day when I momentarily saw myself correctly in the mirror.

Although my physical body healed, and my visual perception eventually was corrected, I had to walk through the transformation of allowing God to heal my self-image. Time spent in His Word helped me learn to see myself the way He sees me—a beautiful, accepted daughter of the One who loves me perfectly.

One of the many lessons I learned from that experience is that I am capable of being deceived. I can be thinking one way, when truth is actually another way. That doesn't cause me to fear; it simply reminds me that my dependence is truly on God and that His Word—His Good News—continually brings my thinking into alignment with His thinking.

The very nature of the Good News is that it is alive and transformational, and we who submit ourselves to it are constantly changed by it. The Good News is that the grace of God is at work in our lives, not just at conversion but in all aspects of our growth in Christian maturity. The apostle Paul wrote in his letter to the Colossian believers: "*This same Good News that came to you is going out all over the world. It is bearing fruit everywhere by changing lives, just as it changed your lives from the day you first heard and understood the truth about God's wonderful grace*" (Colossians 1:6).

The grace of God, through the power of the Gospel, is transforming us day by day as we yield ourselves to Him. Our human nature would prefer that we declare ourselves as having *arrived* when we make the decision of salvation, but in God's Kingdom, that all-important decision is simply the starting point. We are people in need of a lifetime of transformation because we are human. And His Word is our lifeline for true transformation.

There's something in us—namely pride and self-sufficiency—that wants to accumulate experiences and material assets that make our lives feel successful and comfortable when God is working overtime in our lives to highlight our weaknesses and uproot our comfort. Why would He do that? Because our greatest strength comes from admitting our weaknesses. He himself is our strength, but we can't tap into His abundance until we willingly admit our deficiency. The shedding of our pride and self-sufficiency through developing true dependence on Him gives His grace a wide berth in our lives to change us. His grace not only changes us, but through us, His grace is reaching others in ever-widening circles of influence from our lives.

God's grace displayed through our lives is derived from our willingness to assume a posture of weakness. Much like the moment I saw myself correctly in the mirror, I chose to humbly submit my well-being to my mother's care. Most of the leadership training I've encountered has focused on building on our strengths and shoring up our weaknesses. God's grace, however, capitalizes on the very weaknesses we so often try to mend and cover up. For instance, a respected leader in the church who is a father of four children and a husband of thirty years is quietly hiding that he struggled with pornography for years—since he was a young teen. Although free of the addiction now, the guilt and shame still haunt his heart. The years he perceives as wasted are potentially the gift of grace he can offer to others who are struggling with a similar sin. But he must be willing to be vulnerable—to show his weakness—by telling his story of God's grace which has freed him from bondage.

Or perhaps a young CEO secretly struggles with her self-image and feelings of insecurity as she stands in front of the board of directors defending her decision to take the company in a new direction. To appear less than confident would be unacceptable, so she assumes a role that leaves her feeling like an imposter.

Leading well with our weaknesses exposed rather than hidden can actually be a success story in the making.

When we're telling our stories and exposing our weaknesses, simply recounting the history of our sin and brokenness is not the magic touch that heals us; it's actually the posture of humility that enacts our growth and healing process. Our society is so fixated on making ourselves look good that we can take a story of sin and brokenness transformed by God's grace and market it for the purpose of making us wealthy. I'm all about God using our mess to make something beautiful, but we must be cautious that we've taken a humble posture before the Lord. Otherwise, we've made *marketing our mess* all about us...again.

When we allow God to have full control of our lives, revealing our weaknesses to the people around us isn't nearly as threatening as when we are trying to manage our own reputations. Left to ourselves, we'll do most anything to make ourselves look good. But left in God's hands, He'll use our brokenness and weaknesses to display His glorious grace.

There is so much beauty in something that was broken being made whole. I wrote a story about the beautiful process of moving from brokenness to newness in a devotional book I wrote, *Seeds of Faith* (published by Dream Releaser Publishing), and I'll share the story again here.

Many years ago, my mom handed me an early Christmas gift—a beautiful ornament to hang on my tree. It was a transparent glass-blown orb of blue and pink pastels that danced with beauty against the Christmas lights. As captivating as the ornament was, it was my mother's explanation of its history and significance that solidified its importance to me.

In 1980, Mount St. Helens shook in a violent volcanic eruption that resulted in massive damage. In fact, it was deemed the most destructive volcanic eruption in the history of the United States. The spewing lava left a destructive wake of thirteen miles in all directions from the volcanic center. Everything in that circumference of destruction was burned beyond restoration. However, it was from this desolate landscape that my beautiful Christmas ornament had its beginnings.

Ashes from Mount St. Helens were given to glass blowers, who carefully crafted lovely reminders that beauty truly can come from ashes. As my mom handed me the ornament so many years ago, she said, "Debbie, you'll go through things in your life that will seem devastating—beyond restoration. But always remember that God can take those ashes and create beauty. It may not look like it did before, but somehow, when He is finished carefully crafting something new, you'll be pleased with His work."

Tears well up in my eyes as I think about her words to me. Although she's been with Jesus for some time now, I can still hear her voice. And she was right. God has a way of making beauty from ashes. I echo King David's words in Psalm 30: "*You have turned my mourning into joyful dancing. You have taken away my clothes of mourning and clothed me with joy, that I might sing praises to you and not be silent. O Lord my God, I will give you thanks forever!"* (vv. 11-12).

We have the tendency to cover our brokenness and hide it away—carefully cloaking our weaknesses. But that is a disservice to the Body of Christ. How will others find their way out of the darkness of sin and brokenness unless we're willing to show our own vulnerability and offer our empathy?

The very nature of the Good News is that God willingly enters our brokenness and, by His grace, brings beauty out of our messes. We cheapen His Gift when we attempt to mask our weaknesses. The apostle Paul understood that capitalizing on his strengths was unproductive. He chose to lean into his weaknesses and allow *God's strength* to work through him.

> *If I wanted to boast, I would be no fool in doing so, because I would be telling the truth. But I won't do it, because I don't want anyone to give me credit beyond what they can see in my life or hear in my message, even though I have received such wonderful revelations from God. So to keep me from becoming proud, I was given a thorn in my flesh, a messenger from Satan to torment me and keep me from becoming proud. Three different times I begged the Lord to take it away. Each time he said, "My grace is all you need. My power works best in weakness." So now I am glad to boast about my weaknesses, so that the power of Christ can work through me.* (2 Corinthians 12:6-9)

The Lord himself said that His power works best in weakness —both through the Sovereign God himself becoming human flesh and the frailty of our own human condition. So why do we keep trying to appear strong and hide our weaknesses?

We innately want to control our own lives, and we don't want others to perceive that we are not strong. The Gospel constantly challenges us to live opposite the world's ways of doing things. In God's Kingdom, human weakness is not disdained. In fact, according to Paul's words in the verses above, it's celebrated. So when we stop trying to look good, and instead posture ourselves in humility, we begin to experience a shift in how we relate to others. God's strength shines through our lives, and our influence expands. God's marketing strategy works so much better than man's efforts! There is just One God, and He is the only One whose glory and grace should be displayed through our lives.

Chapter 9

REMEMBRANCE

One of the greatest gifts God has given humankind is a mind that can not only process and reason but can remember and choose to act on those remembrances. Memory can serve us well, reminding us of good experiences and painful experiences, as well as those experiences that are best not repeated.

My grandchildren give me plenty of wonderful memories, some endearing and some rather humorous. I recall when my granddaughter Tia was about eighteen months old, I lifted her up to put her in the child seat in my car, and I accidently bumped her head on the doorframe. Tears welled up in her eyes, and I profusely apologized for bumping her head. For probably six months after that incident, EVERY time I started to put her in my car, the dialog would go something like this:

Tia: "Tia bump *her head.*"

Mimi: "Yes, Baby, I'm so sorry about that. But I will be very careful. I won't bump your head *this time.*

Tia: (dramatic pause and purposeful eye-lock) "Tia *is brave.*"

Mimi: "Yes, Baby, Tia *is brave*."

I would then pick her up and successfully deposit her in her seat, at which point she would exclaim, "We did it!" And I would rejoice with her.

Sidenote: In case you're wondering, Tia began talking very early and could carry on conversations by the age of two years old. The entire family has been amazed at her early verbal acuity.

I truly wish she could have forgotten that I had bumped her head, but I realize that the same ability to forget that incident would be the same ability to forget the looks of love between us and the silly things we've laughed about together.

The ability to remember and act upon those remembrances is crucial to our maturity in our Christian walk and to our relational development with others. The ability to remember helps us both process our painful experiences and enjoy our victorious moments.

Oftentimes in counseling, thinking about experiences in the past is the catalyst for our healing. Our most painful wounds are often buried so deep inside us that we've seemingly forgotten about them. But it is through remembering that they can be brought to the surface and dealt with in a way that produces healing.

My husband's little brother was killed by a drunk driver when my husband was just four years old. He and his brother Jerry—who was three years old at the time—were playing in the quiet cul-de-sac of a friend's house. A drunk driver rounded the corner, and before anyone could respond, Jerry was hit and died shortly thereafter. My husband saw the whole tragic event unfold, almost in slow-motion. That was nearly fifty years ago, and no one thought to offer counseling to a four-year-old child. Unfortunately, my husband dealt with repressed relationship issues for years. It affected not only his relationships with other people but also with God.

Never truly grieving that loss nor working his way through his own subsequent issues hindered God's healing in his life for many years. We've been married for nearly forty years, and each time I've asked about the incident, he says he remembers very little about that day. I know that the memories are there; they're just seemingly too painful to fully retrieve. Our minds have a way of repressing traumatic memories that are too difficult to dwell on.

As I think back over my own life, I have so many wonderful memories of my childhood and teenage years. I remember homes we lived in and vacations we took as a family. I remember the churches I grew up in, and the friends' houses I played in. Then as young adults carefree and in love, my husband and I married when we were barely nineteen years old. Our children came along a few years later, and we now have the pleasure of enjoying our grandchildren. They are truly the crowning glory of life!

But not all my memories are pleasant. I remember many of my own physical health incidents: a poisonous cyst that almost took my life at four years old; unresolved stomach ulcers that robbed me of two years of childhood play; anorexia that sought to overtake me at thirteen years old; unexplainable chronic back pain that drove me to my knees as an adult. And yet, my overriding memory is of God's deliverance in each of those experiences.

As a child, I lost two childhood friends four years apart—one to a drunk driver (we were eight years old) and the other to a brain aneurysm (we were twelve years old). I remember standing at their caskets trying to make sense of their deaths. The stuffed animals we had played with adorned their caskets. And yet, the overriding memory is of God's comfort and nearness in each of those experiences.

Each of us has memories that seemingly would be so much easier to forget than to unpack, and to slog our way through the pain feels insurmountable. But if we're going to heal, we need to *remember*. Our relational maturity depends on it. Where we close off parts of ourselves from past hurts, we also close off parts of ourselves that relate well to others.

God reminds us through His Word that our memories are an important part of both our own maturity and the maturity of those we're discipling.

He challenges us to remember His sacrificial love for us: "*But God showed his great love for us by sending Christ to die for us while we were still sinners*" (Romans 5:8).

> *On the night when he was betrayed, the Lord Jesus took some bread and gave thanks to God for it. Then he broke it in pieces and said, 'This is my body, which is given for you. Do this in remembrance of me.' In the same way, he took the cup of wine after supper, saying, "This cup is the new covenant between God and his people—an agreement confirmed with my blood. Do this in remembrance of me as often as you drink it."*
>
> (1 Corinthians 11:23b-25)

He challenges us to remember His precepts: "*You must love the* Lord *your God and always obey his requirements, decrees, regulations, and commands*" (Deuteronomy 11:1).

And He challenges us to remember His miraculous interventions. Although there are many examples of this in Scripture, we'll look at one Old Testament story in particular. As the children of Israel were preparing to enter the Promised Land,

Moses took them on a mental journey through their forty-year history in the wilderness after coming out of Egypt. Moses would not be joining them as they crossed over into the land, so he gave them as many reminders as he possibly could about how the Lord intervened on their behalf. They were about to face people groups they would have to engage in battle, and Moses reminded them not to be afraid based on their history with God.

> *Perhaps you will think to yourselves, "How can we ever conquer these nations that are so much more powerful than we are?" But don't be afraid of them! Just* ***remember*** *what the* LORD *your God did to Pharaoh and to all the land of Egypt.* ***Remember*** *the great terrors the* LORD *your God sent against them. You saw it all with your own eyes! And* ***remember*** *the miraculous signs and wonders, and the strong hand and powerful arm with which he brought you out of Egypt. The* LORD *your God will use this same power against all the people you fear .* (Deuteronomy 7:17-19, emphasis mine)

Moses continued his discourse by reminding the children of Israel how God had miraculously provided for them in the wilderness.

> ***Remember*** *how the* LORD *your God led you through the wilderness for these forty years, humbling you and testing you to prove your character, and to find out whether or not you would obey his commands. Yes, he humbled you by letting you go hungry and then feeding you with manna, a food previously unknown to you and your ancestors. He did it to teach you that people do not live by bread alone; rather, we live by every word that comes from the mouth of the* LORD. *For all these forty years your clothes didn't wear out, and your feet didn't blister or swell.* ***Think about it.*** *Just as a parent*

> *disciplines a child, the* Lord *your God disciplines you for your own good.* (Deuteronomy 8:2-5, emphasis mine)

The children of Israel were facing new challenges and learning to rely on God's love for them and His power to intervene on their behalf. Their fear certainly drove them to cry out to God and taught them that God's intervention in their lives was a necessary part of their existence. God hears those prayers of fear, and He desires to bring comfort and victory as He teaches us to depend on Him.

But once the Israelites had settled in their new land, they would face a different enemy—comfort and self-reliance. We tend to do the same thing today. When we are under great pressure, we remember to cry out to God and beg His intervention. But when all is peaceful, we tend toward comfort and self-reliance if we aren't careful.

My mother often challenged me in unique ways as I was growing up—even into my adult years. I clearly remember one admonition she used to give me, "Remaining faithful to the Lord is easier when you are desperately in need of Him than when you are walking in abundance. Beware of self-reliance in your comfort and success." Although her warning felt a bit misplaced in my young life, my heightened awareness of that particular human tendency over the years alerted me to what the Word of God has to say about our success. Moses gave the same type of warning to the people of Israel:

> *For the* Lord *your God is bringing you into a good land of flowing streams and pools of water, with fountains and springs that gush out in the valleys and hills. It is a land of wheat and barley; of grapevines, fig trees, and pomegranates; of olive oil and honey. It is a land where food is plentiful and*

> *nothing is lacking. It is a land where iron is as common as stone, and copper is abundant in the hills. When you have eaten your fill,* ***be sure*** *to praise the* LORD *your God for the good land he has given you.*
>
> *But that is the time to* ***be careful! Beware*** *that in your plenty you do not forget the* LORD *your God and disobey his commands, regulations, and decrees that I am giving you today. For when you have become full and prosperous and have built fine homes to live in, and when your flocks and herds have become very large and your silver and gold have multiplied along with everything else,* ***be careful!*** *Do not become proud at that time and forget the* LORD *your God, who rescued you from the slavery in the land of Egypt.*
>
> (Deuteronomy 8:7-14, emphasis mine)

I wish I could say that such a clear warning would prevent them and us from moving into the comfort and self-reliance of our abundance, but I think the shift happens so slowly that we sort of drift away from relying closely on the Lord. So how do we remain dependent on the One who sustains us? Remembrance.

When we deliberately dwell on who He is, what He has done, and how He has intervened time and time again in our lives, our hearts swell with gratitude, and we draw near to Him once again. I'll close this chapter with a beautiful passage that calls us to remembrance.

> *For the* LORD *your God is the God of gods and Lord of lords. He is the great God, the mighty and awesome God, who shows no partiality and cannot be bribed. He ensures that orphans and widows receive justice. He shows love to the foreigners living among you and gives them food and clothing. So you, too, must show love to foreigners, for* ***you yourselves***

> ***were once foreigners in the land of Egypt****. You must* ***fear the LORD your God*** *and* ***worship him*** *and* ***cling to him****. Your oaths must be in his name alone.* ***He alone is your God, the only one who is worthy of your praise, the one who has done these mighty miracles that you have seen with your own eyes.*** (Deuteronomy 10:17-21, emphasis mine)

Chapter 10

UNITY

The supernatural power of heaven is available to us to the degree that we grasp and implement such important concepts as unity. So much of what God wants to do in the earth is done through the unity of His people. And we forego much of His available power when we fiercely value our independence.

The Scriptures have much to say about how we are to relate to one another and work together for the purposes of God's Kingdom. The way God interacts with us as individuals and as a people is based on covenant—covenant through the salvation relationship, through people groups, and through marriage. Let me explain.

The beautiful relationship that we are offered with Christ as individuals comes through covenant relationship. God was the initiator of the covenant through Christ. God sent His Son to earth to take our sin upon himself and become our sacrificial atonement so we could be in His presence, righteous and pure. The apostle Paul reminds us of God's gift to us in his letter to the Christians at Ephesus, *"He is so rich in kindness and grace that he purchased our freedom with the blood of his Son and forgave our sins*" (Ephesians 1:7). What an amazing act of kindness!

We then respond to God's offer to us to enter into covenant relationship with Him. The terms of the covenant were initiated by Him, spelled out by Him in His Word, and carried out by Him. Our part of the covenant is to respond to His merciful offer and then to decidedly live by the terms (His Word) He set forth. When we do this, we are unified with Him in a supernatural and inseparable bond called salvation.

But God didn't just want to save us as individuals; He wanted a group of people who would represent Him and His offer of salvation to a dying world. This plan began with Abraham and his descendants—the children of Israel. And it continues with anyone who will respond to His offer of salvation. There is supernatural power that accompanies a group of people unified in Christ—whether that's a family, a church, a city, a state, a nation, or a group of nations.

Supernatural unity isn't based on people getting together to simply accomplish a goal; it's based on Holy Spirit-empowered believers setting their focus on Christ. And He himself fills the sacred space between us, creating a whole, unified Body. We mistakenly believe that if we set the right goals or create an exceptionally attractive project, people will unify around us to achieve great things for God. But then we end up doing good projects hoping God is onboard with *our* plans, rather than achieving God-ordained purposes into which *He has invited us.* Unity comes when we collectively set our eyes on Him and choose to participate in what *He is doing*. And that kind of unity is what changes families, churches, cities, states, and nations.

Now let's talk about the idea of unity in marriage. Marriage by God's design is a revealed example of how unity in salvation works and how unity on a larger scale—within churches and people groups—functions. Because of our human tendency toward fierce independence, unity in marriage is truly a sacrificial act of humility. Unity in marriage is more than two people living in the same household; it's a decision by both husband and wife to set their hearts on the things of God and consistently turn their gaze toward Christ. Then He fills the sacred space between husband and wife, creating power in their unified position in Christ.

Disunity—whether in marriages, families, churches, communities, or nations—diminishes and/or disengages the availability of God's supernatural power. This state of diminished or disengaged power has significant and catastrophic effects on families, churches, communities, and nations.

I think we have a hard time grasping the magnitude of the power we forego because we so rarely see it functioning the way God intended. For an example of beautiful unity that disintegrated into disunity, let's look in the Old Testament at the reign of King Solomon over all Israel.

At the beginning of King Solomon's reign, "*The people of Judah and Israel were as numerous as the sand on the seashore. They were very contented, with plenty to eat and drink...During the lifetime of Solomon, all of Judah and Israel lived in peace and safety. And from Dan in the north to Beersheba in the south, each family had its own home and garden*" (1 Kings 4:20, 25).

But by the time we get to the end of Solomon's life:

> *He had 700 wives of royal birth and 300 concubines. And in fact, they did turn his heart away from the* Lord*. In Solomon's old age, they turned his heart to worship other gods* ***instead of being completely faithful to the* Lord *his God****, as his father, David, had been... So now the* Lord *said to him, "Since you have not kept my covenant and have disobeyed*

> *my decrees, I will surely tear the kingdom away from you and give it to one of your servants. But for the sake of your father, David, I will not do this while you are still alive. I will take the kingdom away from your son."*
>
> (1 Kings 11:3-4, 11-12, emphasis mine)

Through Solomon's broken covenant with God, his own family was decimated, the people of Israel were provoked to idol worship, the nation was divided, and generations were forever altered. King Solomon lost his focus on the true Source of unity, and the consequences were monumental.

If those are tragic consequences of losing focus on God and creating disunity, then what are the positive consequences of initiating and maintaining unity of focus on Him?

As we set our eyes on the Lord, we operate in greater love toward one another. The value of human life—as God views us—is elevated, and we operate in cooperation with one another much more easily. What we can accomplish together is so much greater than what we can do alone.

As we experience unity, a greater level of peace resides over our communities and our families. We then have margin to rest properly and enjoy higher levels of creativity that are often stilted during the chaos of disunity. Out of creativity comes ideas to solve problems that make life more enjoyable and more fulfilling. Creativity tends to leak from our lives in almost imperceptible amounts during times of conflict and crisis until it's gone completely. We find ourselves functioning in isolation just trying to "get it all done," and life becomes monotonous and exhausting.

The Bible clearly teaches us that Satan comes to steal, kill, and destroy. Jesus' presence in us brings life and that life more abundantly! Disunity and discord are Satan's attempt to interrupt the flow of God's blessings in our lives, our families, our churches, and our nations. His goal is to draw our gaze away from the Lord and encourage us to put it on ourselves. Once we're focused on our own needs, we begin to see the people around us as objects to be opposed rather than God's gifts of camaraderie.

The enemy of our souls knows what we are capable of when we are united under the Lordship of Jesus Christ. We have the authority of Christ available to us as we focus on Him, and when we access that authority in community, Kingdom power is present to change lives, impact cities, and influence nations. No wonder Satan works overtime to sow discord among us.

The apostle Paul implored the Christians at Ephesus to remain united both for benefit in the present as well as in eternity.

> *Make every effort to keep yourselves united in the Spirit, binding yourselves together with peace. For there is one body and one Spirit, just as you have been called to one glorious hope for the future.* (Ephesians 4:3-4)

And what is that glorious hope for the future?

> *After this I saw a vast crowd, too great to count, from every nation and tribe and people and language, standing in front of the throne and before the Lamb. They were clothed in white robes and held palm branches in their hands. And they were shouting with a great roar, "Salvation comes from our God who sits on the throne and from the Lamb!"*
>
> (Revelation 7:9-10)

When we stand before God's throne in Heaven, there will be no divisions of people groups or purpose. We have one purpose—to exalt the Holy One of Israel. We are one body—united under the Lordship of Jesus Christ. And there is only One God—just One!

ALSO AVAILABLE FROM BRIDGE-LOGOS

WHEN GOD SPEAKS

Deborah Stricklin

Hearing the voice of our Savior is a great gift—a gift to be treasured and cultivated. His voice brings life to our seemingly lifeless situations. And as God speaks, He reveals more of himself, enabling us to view our lives from His bounty of resources and power. Those situations in life that leave us feeling limited and downtrodden become opportunities for the voice of God to create through us, clarify purpose in us, and challenge us to think differently. Learning to hear His voice more clearly requires intentional discipline and humble obedience. But He desires to speak to each one of us and is committed to helping us learn to listen. He always finishes what He starts, and He has empowered us through His words to join Him in His plans and purposes in the earth. There is no greater privilege than to partner with the Almighty God. Let's train our hearts to hear His voice as He leads us forward.

ISBN: 9780-1-61036-916-9

ALSO AVAILABLE FROM BRIDGE-LOGOS

KEEP YOUR EYES ON ME

Deborah Stricklin

Learning to keep your eyes on Jesus is not easy. When circumstances get difficult, we naturally want to focus on the problem, turning it over and over in our minds until we arrive at some sort of solution. The Lord is inviting us to set our eyes on Him regardless of the circumstances. And as we focus on Him, He brings resolution. That resolution may simply be peace in the middle of the difficulty, but peace with Him gives us the ability to navigate even the most challenging circumstances.

Forty days is long enough to establish a new pattern in our thinking, but to become truly comfortable living in the ambiguity of unresolved problems or threatening circumstances takes purposeful effort in keeping our eyes heavenward over a long period of time. Jesus is eager to teach us how to navigate life with our eyes on Him. And then, trust in the One who is leading us grows with each passing day.

ISBN: 978-1-61036-922-0

www.ingramcontent.com/pod-product-compliance
Lightning Source LLC
LaVergne TN
LVHW020653100826
845148LV00012B/2476

* 9 7 8 1 6 1 0 3 6 9 2 4 4 *